EVOCATIVE STYLE

KELLY
WEARSTLER

WITH **RIMA SUQI**

EVOCATIVE STYLE

RIZZOLI
NEW YORK

New York · Paris · London · Milan

CONTENTS

The environments featured within this book represent a continual evolution and refinement of my design aesthetic, philosophy and development. Each project was personal, unique, and presented an opportunity to share my passion for history, the arts, and established as well as emerging artists and artisans, with clients who were open and engaged. Inspirations were infinite—from the simple beauty found in nature to fashion runways and street style, from the structured tenets of graphic design to the rich traditions of decorative arts and the innovative use of technology. Each space provided an opportunity to challenge personal and professional boundaries, celebrate the atypical and unexpected, and create multifaceted interiors that are at once inviting and alive with history, culture, and modernity.

————————

KELLY WEARSTLER

Art de Vivre

A 1901 Beaux-Arts limestone town house just off Central Park, in New York, boasted a significant architectural heritage, which is evident from the stately exterior. The interior, however, had been separated over the decades into both commercial and residential spaces, and was in the depths of an identity crisis. A gut renovation ensued.

The couple who purchased the then five-story townhome are art enthusiasts with an extensive and important collection, as well as avid entertainers who routinely host dinners where twenty or more people can be found around the dining table. They are a young family, and their home needed to reflect a modern sensibility without completely ignoring the formality of the building's architecture.

Moldings weren't banished but were reduced to a minimal yet thoughtfully placed role; a subtle one-inch bronze reveal was inserted where ceiling meets walls, solid wood doors were crafted from stained walnut, and an entire floor was added to the home, creating a rooftop garden room flanked by two terraces, with industrial architectural details inspired by Jean Prouvé.

The resulting home is an extremely sophisticated mélange of styles ranging from Chinese art deco to European mid-century masters, and contemporary emerging artists that is both inspired and incredibly welcoming.

A NEW, SCULPTURAL STAIRCASE WITH A SEXY CURVE WAS ADDED TO THE
HOME, WHILE THE WALLS ALONGSIDE IT WERE BEAUTIFULLY BURNISHED
USING PLASTER OF PARIS. A PRISTINE 1940S CHINESE ART DECO RUG
IN VIBRANT SHADES OF ORANGE, FUCHSIA, AND GREEN WAS REPURPOSED
AS A STAIR RUNNER AND ADDS A JOLT OF COLOR IN AN OTHERWISE
MINIMAL SPACE. ITALIAN STALWARTS WERE SOURCED FOR LIGHTING: AN
ELEGANT 1940S MURANO GLASS CHANDELIER SPEAKS TO THE ARC OF THE
STAIRCASE AND A SET OF RARE FRANCO ALBINI LINEAR BRASS SCONCES
FOLLOW THAT CURVE FOR SEVERAL FLOORS.

A VINTAGE ITALIAN WINGED ARMCHAIR, SET BENEATH A PAINTING BY AMERICAN ARTIST DAN COLEN, SEEMS TO BE IN CONVERSATION WITH A WOODEN ROBOT. THAT WHIMSICAL PIECE OPENS TO REVEAL THAT IT IS A "MOBILE BAR," DESIGNED IN 1969 BY BORGHESANI, WHO WAS ALLEGEDLY INSPIRED BY THE LUNAR LANDING.

A PAIR OF 1960S MAISON JANSEN ARMCHAIRS
FLANK A HELLA JONGERIUS GEMSTONE SIDE TABLE
WITH A GRAPHITE PAINTING BY ADAM MCEWEN AS
AN ELEGANT BACKDROP.

A NEWLY DESIGNED SECRET DOOR UNDERNEATH A STAIRCASE LANDING
OPENS TO REVEAL A WALK-IN BAR, MAKING EXCELLENT USE OF WHAT
WOULD OTHERWISE BE NEGATIVE SPACE, ESPECIALLY FOR A COUPLE
THAT HOSTS LARGE WEEKLY DINNERS. A PAIR OF ETTORE SOTTSASS
DEMISTELLA TABLES ACTS AS SENTRIES GUARDING THE ENTRANCE; THE
BURNISHED BRASS BANNISTER WAS CUSTOM DESIGNED FOR THE HOME.

A SETH PRICE PIECE IS HUNG OVER AN ENAMELED
LACQUERED CRAB CABINET BY FRENCH CONTEMPORARY
ARTIST ROLAND MELLAN.

THIS PAGE: IN A CORNER OF THE DINING ROOM, TWO MINIMALIST MASTERS HOLD COURT IN THE FORM OF A RARE CURVACEOUS BRONZE CHAIR BY PAUL EVANS, SET BESIDE A BRONZE AND LINEN WALL LIGHT BY FELIX AGOSTINI, BOTH FROM THE 1960S. THE CUSTOM PARQUET FLOORING IS A WOVEN DESIGN INCORPORATING EBONY, OAK, AND WALNUT WOODS.

PREVIOUS PAGE: IN THE DINING ROOM, A CUSTOM-DESIGNED WHITE OAK TABLE WITH A TONAL VENEER TOP IS ARTFULLY ARRANGED WITH A SELECTION OF VINTAGE FRENCH AND ITALIAN CHAIRS FROM THE 1940S, '50S, AND '60S. A PAIR OF 1970S CANDELABRAS BY VICTOR ROMAN, A ROMANIAN SCULPTOR, FLANK A WORK BY INTERDISCIPLINARY ARTIST NATE LOWMAN, HUNG ABOVE A 1970S FRENCH SIDEBOARD.

THE KITCHEN CABINETS, HOOD, AND REFRIGERATOR ARE ALL
CLAD IN PATINATED BRASS, GIVING THE SUBTERRANEAN ROOM
A WARM GLOW. A PAIR OF SNAKE BARSTOOLS WERE CUSTOM MADE
FOR THE SPACE AND NESTLE UNDERNEATH A GENEROUS, MARBLE-
TOPPED CENTER ISLAND, WHICH ALSO HOLDS A HANDCRAFTED
FOOTED BOWL BY ETTORE SOTTSASS FOR BITOSSI. SOURCES OF
LIGHT ARE ALL SET IN THE CEILING, AND INCLUDE OPALINE
HAND-BLOWN GLASS PENDANTS IN THE STYLE OF WIENER
WERKSTÄTTE. THE BLACK-AND-WHITE CHECKERBOARD FLOOR WAS
INSPIRED BY VIENNESE COFFEEHOUSES.

AN INFORMAL DINING AREA IN A CORNER OF THE KITCHEN, WITH
VINTAGE JACQUES QUINET CHAIRS SET AROUND A CUSTOM BLACKENED
BRASS TABLE WITH A QUIETLY LUXURIOUS TOP INLAID WITH THREE
TYPES OF SEMIPRECIOUS STONES. THE HAND-PAINTED CERAMIC PLATES
ARE FROM THE *DINNER FOR ANIMALS* SERIES, CREATED BY ARTIST
NICOLAS PARTY. THE BRUTALIST-STYLE CREDENZA IS A VINTAGE PIECE
BY AN UNKNOWN DESIGNER; IT IS USED FOR STORAGE AND TO DISPLAY
THE OWNER'S PERSONAL COLLECTION OF SOTTSASS TEAPOTS. A LADIES
AND GENTLEMAN STUDIO SHAPE UP CHANDELIER ECHOES THE SHAPES AND
COLORS OF THOSE TEAPOTS, WHILE PROVIDING A SCULPTURAL SOURCE
OF LIGHT.

THIS PAGE: THE CABINET SHOWN AT LEFT IS THE BRAINCHILD OF LOS ANGELES–BASED ARTIST PETER SHIRE, WHO WAS AN ORIGINAL MEMBER OF THE MEMPHIS GROUP, A DESIGN COLLECTIVE FOUNDED BY ETTORE SOTTSASS IN 1980 THAT IS CURRENTLY EXPERIENCING A MAJOR RESURGENCE. THE CABINET IS SET IN A NOOK IN THE SUBTERRANEAN FAMILY ROOM, BELOW A LARGE FORMAT TROLL POLAROID BY BERKELEY–BASED ARTIST LUTZ BACHER.

NEXT PAGE: THE MASTER SUITE ENTRANCE AREA IS ANCHORED BY A RARE (ONE OF THIRTY) MARBLE AND GILT DEL DIAVOLO MIRROR BY ETTORE SOTTSASS, CIRCA 1980. IT STANDS IN OPPOSITION TO SMALL KNOTTY BUBBLE PENDANT LAMPS OF MOUTH–BLOWN GLASS WITH NATURAL WHITE ROPE BY LINDSEY ADELMAN STUDIO.

THE MASTER BATH IS AN ODE TO NATURAL MATERIALS IN
THEIR MOST GLAMOROUS INCARNATIONS. PATINATED BRASS
DIVIDED LIGHT DOORS FRAME RIBBED GLASS, WALLS
ARE CLAD IN LUMINESCENT GLASS TILES, AND VINTAGE
SMOKED GLASS SCONCES, ETCHED WITH A WAVE MOTIF,
ILLUMINATE THE SPACE.

A CUSTOM-DESIGNED UPHOLSTERED LEATHER BED, IN A
SOOTHING SHADE OF BLUE, ANCHORS A YOUNG GIRL'S
LIGHT-FILLED, SOUTH-FACING BEDROOM. THE DESK IS
ALSO A CUSTOM PIECE, PAIRED WITH A CHAIR DESIGNED
BY PIERO LISSONI IN THE 1960S AND A SOTTSASS LAMP
FROM THE OWNER'S PERSONAL COLLECTION.

THE BEST TYPE OF LIP SERVICE: A CUSTOM—DESIGNED BED INSPIRED
BY AN ICONIC 1930S SALVADOR DALÍ SOFA IN THE SHAPE OF MAE
WEST'S LIPS. THE REDDISH TONES OF THE BED CARRY OVER TO THE
F/K/A LAMPS BY MULTIDISCIPLINARY DESIGNER JONAH TAKAGI, THE
VINTAGE CHANDELIER, THE CUSTOM—DESIGNED LAMINATE DESK AND
THE SOTTSASS TABLE LAMP.

REPEATING GEOMETRIC PATTERNS UNITE THE DESIGN OF THEIR SON'S
ROOM, FROM THE NIGHTSTAND TO THE EDWARD FIELDS RUG, THE VINTAGE
MARIO BOTTA SHOGUN LAMP, AND THE VINTAGE SWIVEL CHAIRS BY
GIANNI MOSCATELLI UPHOLSTERED IN A PATTERNED LEATHER.

A FLOOR WAS ADDED TO THE HOME AND MADE INTO A SITTING AREA
WITH JEAN PROUVÉ-INSPIRED INDUSTRIAL DETAILS IN THE FORM
OF EXPOSED METAL CEILING BEAMS AND CASEMENT WINDOWS. A
CONTEMPORARY BDDW ABEL SOFA IS FLANKED BY 1970S BELGIAN
FLOOR LAMPS, A 1960S ITALIAN GLASS CHAIR, AND A SLATE
CIRCULAR COFFEE TABLE ENCRUSTED WITH AGATE SLICES.

A COMMANDING CABINET CUSTOM CRAFTED FROM MULTIDIRECTIONAL
RIBBED WALNUT CONCEALS THE TELEVISION AND BAR. IT SHARES
THE SPACE WITH A VINTAGE FRENCH SIDE TABLE AND FABIO LENCI'S
ICONIC HYALINE GLASS CHAIR.

Vintage Voltage

There are interiors that inspire the minute they are presented as a blank canvas, and others where more imagination is required to see through a maze of imperfections and recognize a space's ultimate potential. While the results might suggest otherwise, this home, in its former incarnation, was the latter: a California bungalow, complete with brown ceiling beams and stark white walls that had been renovated and expanded into a sprawling modern home with an open but oddly fragmented floor plan.

Creating a cohesive space began with paring down the unseemly details that had been added by previous owners, and adding subtle but significant architectural elements that were more authentic to the style of the home. The entry was transformed from a traditional rectangular door into a graceful, welcoming arch and the open doorways of the kitchen and dining rooms were expanded and framed in dark Portoro marble. Textured linen wallpaper squares were applied to the walls of almost every room in the home, which simultaneously created a cohesive visual narrative while delineating spaces via complementary color palettes in shades of blue, coral, and cream that changed from room to room.

Furnishings span styles and eras, from custom-crafted contemporary pieces to avant-garde, often dramatic forms in exuberant colors, celebrating the client's love of art and sculpture. Many are important pieces attributed to masters the likes of Ettore Sottsass, Verner Panton, and Jean Royère; they mingle with creations from the current generation's standout stars Katie Stout, Misha Kahn, and Anton Alvarez. Personal touches include several rugs custom loomed using imagery from abstract paintings created by one of the owners, who is an artist. Some arrangements may seem contradictory at first, and a challenge to the senses. But the tension created imbues the home with energy, soul, and a plethora of conversation pieces.

THIS PAGE: SLIP-CAST DINNERWARE HANDCRAFTED AND PAINTED BY CERAMICIST DOUG PELTZMAN, WHO FOUNDED HIS UPSTATE NEW YORK STUDIO FIFTEEN YEARS AGO.

PREVIOUS PAGE: THE DINING ROOM WALLS, AS WELL AS MOST WALLS IN THIS HOME, ARE COVERED IN TEXTURED LINEN WALLPAPER SQUARES IN COMPLEMENTARY SHADES. HUNG ON THIS WALL IS *SPRING SUNSET* BY LANA GOMEZ. JAIME HAYON'S REACTION POETIQUE CENTERPIECE, INSPIRED BY THE PICTORIAL WORKS OF LE CORBUSIER, IS SET ATOP A CUSTOMIZED TABLE OF BLEACHED AND EBONIZED OAK, SURROUNDED BY A SET OF 1980S SAPORITI DINING CHAIRS.

(RIGHT) THE ENTRY AND FOYER FEATURE A SERIES OF
CIRCULAR SHAPES—THE LOUVERED WINDOW, CANOE
SCONCES, THE SPECCHIO INFINITO ILLUMINATING
MIRROR, THE DANTE BAVARESK MARBLE TABLE, AND
THE PAINTING BY LEONARD BRENNER. (ABOVE)
EARTHENWARE POSTMODERN SLAB CONSTRUCTION NUDE
SCULPTURE BY HERMAN RODERICK VOLZ.

THIS PAGE: LEONARD BRENNER WAS AN AMERICAN PAINTER WHOSE WORK IS IN THE PERMANENT COLLECTION OF THE GUGGENHEIM. HIS UNTITLED ACRYLIC ON CANVAS, SHOWN HERE, HOLDS A PLACE OF HONOR IN THE ENTRYWAY OF THE HOME. THE LINEN WALLPAPER SQUARES THAT LINE THE WALLS OF THE SPACE WERE CUSTOM COLORED TO COMPLEMENT THIS PIECE AND, CONVENIENTLY, THE 1980S MOSCHINO SEQUINED JACKET DRAPED OVER A CHAIR.

NEXT PAGE: A CUSTOM CABINET BY LOS ANGELES–BASED ARTIST PETER SHIRE, WHO WAS AN ORIGINAL MEMBER OF THE MEMPHIS GROUP, A DESIGN COLLECTIVE FOUNDED BY ETTORE SOTTSASS IN 1980 THAT BECAME KNOWN FOR SOPHISTICATED FUNCTIONAL PIECES IN VIBRANT COLORS WITH A TOUCH OF WHIMSY. ONE OF THE OWNERS OF THIS HOME HAS REFERRED TO SOTTSASS AS HER "SPIRIT ANIMAL."

A 1950S ITALIAN CABINET COVERED IN WHITE AND GOLD MOSAIC
TILES FUNCTIONS AS A GLAMOROUS METALLIC ACCENT IN THE
LIVING ROOM. IT IS SET BENEATH A PAINTING BY LANA GOMEZ
AND A JEAN ROYÈRE TRIPLE ARM SCONCE. THE SOFA AND CHAIRS
ARE CUSTOM DESIGNS.

COLORFUL BANDS AROUND WITH SOFT FOLDS, A PAINTING BY JEAN
ALEXANDER FRATER, SHARES A CORNER WITH A JEAN ROYÈRE
SCONCE, A CABINET BY KATIE STOUT, AND VERNER PANTON'S
COLLECTIBLE VILBERT CHAIR FOR IKEA, WHICH DEBUTED IN 1995.

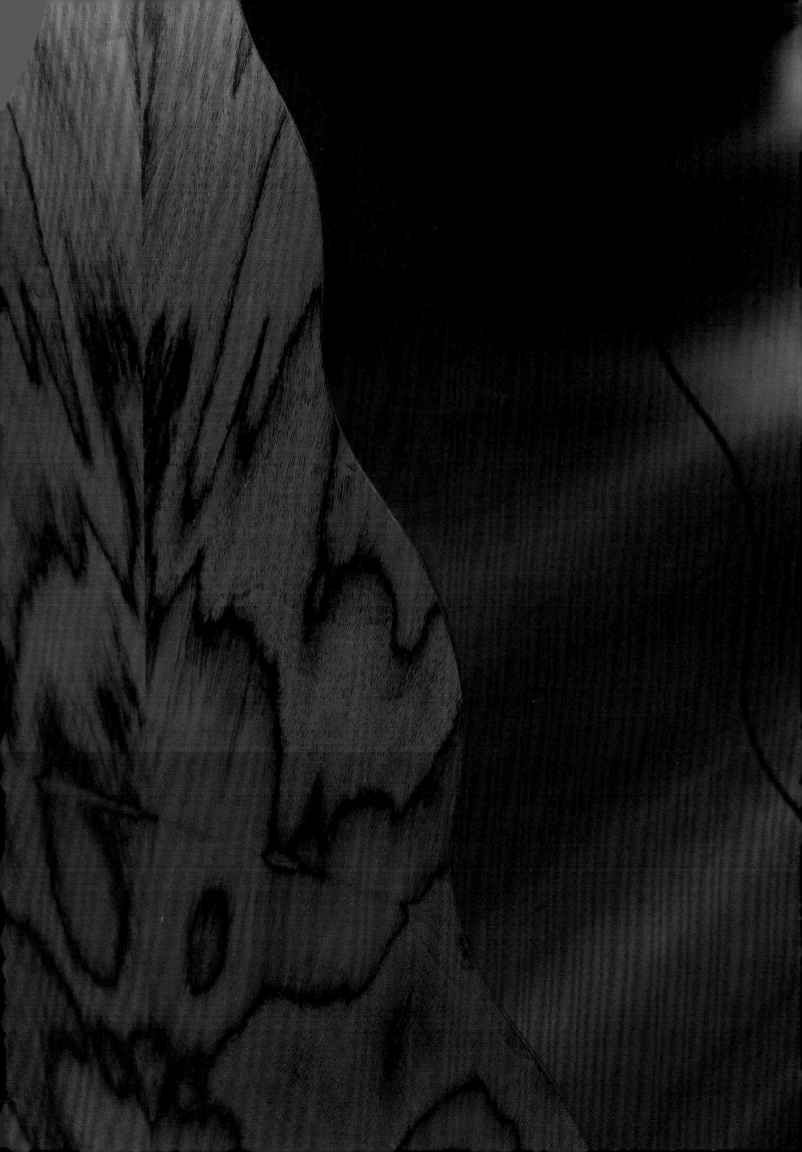

THE SECOND FLOOR LANDING FEATURES AN ICONIC
ETTORE SOTTSASS PIECE: THE SYBILLA, A DESIGN
THAT INCORPORATES A TABLE, MIRROR, AND TWO LAMPS.

A LALA CABINET BY DOKTER AND MISSES STANDS IN GRAPHIC
JUXTAPOSITION TO KATIE STOUT AND SEAN GERSTLEY'S CURVACEOUS
SQUIGGLE LAMP; HUNG ABOVE IS "SKY LIGHT," AN OPTICAL
PAINTED WOOD RELIEF BY MID–CENTURY ARTIST JOHN TOWNSEND.

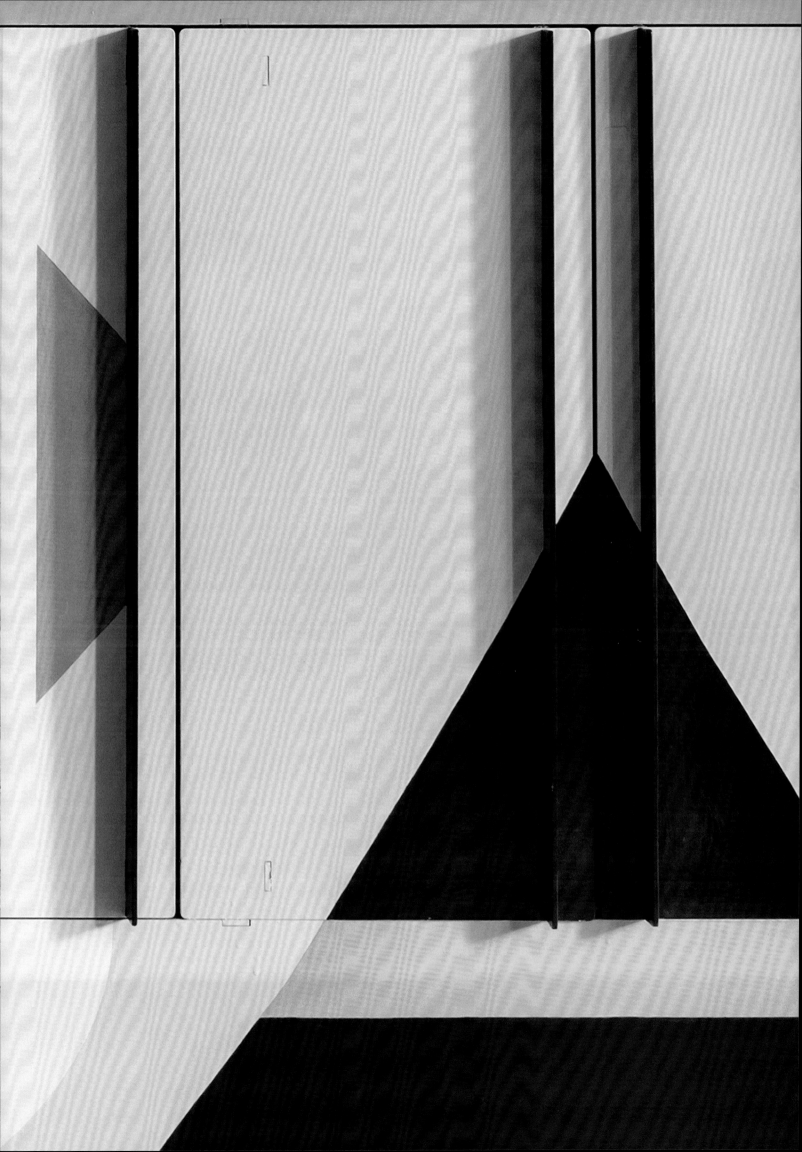

THE CLIENTS HAD A BABY GIRL DURING THE RENOVATION OF THEIR HOME, WHICH
PROVIDED A RARE FIRST: THE OPPORTUNITY TO DESIGN A CRIB, WHICH THE
OWNERS REFERRED TO AS THE "TANK." WHILE THEIR DAUGHTER'S ROOM HAS SOME
SHOTS OF PINK, IT IS AN OF-THE-MOMENT, MEMPHIS-INSPIRED SHADE. A SUR-
PRISINGLY SOPHISTICATED SPACE, IT HAS A FEW PASTEL MOMENTS COURTESY OF
A CLASSIC 1980S MEMPHIS CABINET AND A PSYCHEDELIC OP ART PAINTING HUNG
ABOVE A PINK SLEEPER SOFA. THESE ARE BALANCED BY A BAMBOO SILK RUG IN
NEUTRAL TONES, A CUSTOM-DESIGNED CRIB, AND A CALDER-INSPIRED MOBILE.

THIS PAGE: LOCATED JUST OFF THE ENTRY FOYER, WITH ITS REPEAT OF COLORFUL CIRCULAR SHAPES, IS THE POWDER ROOM, IN THE MOST NEUTRAL OF TONES, WITH NARY A CURVE IN SIGHT. THE SINK AND ITS SURROUND ARE A STRIKING INSTALLATION OF STRIATED STONE INCORPORATING MID-CENTURY BAROVIER & TOSO MURANO GLASS SCONCES. THE MIXED MEDIA PIECE IN THE FOREGROUND IS LEN KLIKUNAS'S *THERE IS A BLOCK IN THE VOID -DARK MESA, 2017.*

NEXT PAGE: THE BACKYARD IS A MULTILEVEL SPACE FEATURING THE REQUISITE POOL (WITH BONUS WATER FEATURE) AND OUTDOOR LIVING ROOM SET WITH CONTEMPORARY, MOSTLY CUSTOM-DESIGNED PIECES COVERED IN PERFORMANCE FABRICS. THE CEMENT SIDE TABLES ARE BY BROOKLYN ARTIST FERNANDO MASTRANGELO, THE BRUTALIST-STYLE CERAMIC PLANTER IN A VERDANT SHADE OF GREEN WAS MADE BY BARI ZIPERSTEIN OF B. ZIPPY DESIGNS IN LOS ANGELES.

Trompe L'oeil Triumph

On a charming SoHo street sits a boutique loft building whose design cleverly masks the fact that it's a relatively new build. There's only one triplex in this building, owned by a couple who call San Francisco home but who are in New York often enough to warrant buying a two-bedroom pied-à-terre. The positives included high ceilings, expansive windows with beautiful city views, and multiple terraces providing incredible outdoor space, a true luxury in this city.

But the eighteen hundred square-foot apartment had an awkward, Jenga-like layout with claustrophobic moments caused by an enclosed switchback staircase that spanned all three floors. Out it went, along with several walls, replaced by a sculptural staircase, a beautiful open bronze spiral that allows for one to stand at its penthouse apex and have an unobstructed view to the base. The curvaceous walls of the staircase are covered from top to bottom with what looks like billowing fabric—and which is based on a photograph of fabric that was actually draped in the space—but is in actuality a hand-painted trompe l'oeil installation and a unifying force that forms the heart of this home.

Intimate rooms were redesigned, emerging from their cocoons to realize their full potential. The kitchen became a brass and marble-clad multifunctional wonder, with Japanese-inspired sliding doors that allow spaces to be selectively hidden from view. Storage, always a concern in urban spaces, is abundant throughout, often camouflaged within desirable vintage and functional art pieces. Emerging artists are featured throughout at the request of the couple, who were interested in building a collection. The resulting design incorporates several classic elements, including a grand staircase and urban terrace, yet is reinvented and refreshed.

THE LIVING ROOM IS A VISUAL HOMAGE TO SIGNIFICANT DESIGN OVER
THE DECADES, ANCHORED BY A CUSTOM CONTEMPORARY SOFA AND A PAIR
OF WARD BENNETT CHAIRS SET AROUND A 1970S BRONZE COFFEE TABLE
BY BELGIAN ARTIST ADO CHALE. TWO UNIQUE WHITE PORCELAIN TULIP
SCULPTURES BY MATTHEW SOLOMON, A BROOKLYN-BORN ARTIST BASED IN
UPSTATE NEW YORK, ARE SET ON THE COFFEE TABLE NEXT TO A 1990S
VASE BY TIM ANDREWS, AN ARTIST KNOWN FOR SMOKE-FIRED AND RAKU
CERAMICS. A CUSTOM RUG DESIGN IN A SATURATED BLUSH TONE ADDS A
POP OF COLOR AND UNIFIES THE SPACE.

EVOCATIVE STYLE

(ABOVE) A BEJEWELED BRASS STOOL WAS CUSTOM CRAFTED WITH STONES INDIVIDUALLY SELECTED, POLISHED, AND SET BY A JEWELER; A CERAMIC FACEPOT BY NEW YORK ARTIST DAN MCCARTHY SITS ON TOP. (RIGHT) THE CLIENT'S REQUEST FOR STORAGE AND SCULPTURE WAS FILLED WITH A TRUE STATEMENT PIECE: A KELLY WEARSTLER-DESIGNED THREE-TIERED BRONZE CABINET, FABRICATED AT A PROMINENT SCULPTOR'S WORKSHOP IN LOS ANGELES, WITH BAKED ENAMEL DRAWERS IN CAREFULLY CHOSEN JEWEL TONES. *JARMAN'S SHINGLE*, A PAINTING BY GILLIAN AYRES, ONE OF ENGLAND'S MOST SIGNIFICANT ABSTRACT ARTISTS, IS HUNG AT LEFT.

A JEWEL BOX OF A POWDER ROOM MAKES THE MOST OF MINIMAL SQUARE FOOTAGE
WITH MOMENTS INCLUDING (LEFT) A CABINET THAT WAS A COLLABORATION
BETWEEN KELLY WEARSTLER AND LOS ANGELES ARTIST PETER SHIRE, SET
WITH A PAIR OF VINTAGE TABLE LAMPS BY SWEDISH DESIGNER HANS-AGNE
JAKOBSSON. HUNG ABOVE IT IS AN OIL PAINTING BY DANIEL CUMMINGS.
THE STONE SLAB SINK VANITY (ABOVE) IS A KELLY WEARSTLER CUSTOM
DESIGN; A VINTAGE 1970S AUSTRIAN GLASS BEAD AND BRASS MIRROR WAS
INSTALLED ABOVE.

THIS LANDING IS ALL ABOUT CURVES (ABOVE): A 1980S
CHAIR BY PARISIAN DREAM TEAM GAROUSTE & BONETTI,
A CONTEMPORARY TRAVERTINE STOOL-AS-SIDE-TABLE BY
SARAH KUENG AND LOVIS CAPUTO, AND THE MAJESTIC ARC
OF THE CUSTOM-DESIGNED BANNISTER AND STAIR RAIL. THE
GUEST BEDROOM (RIGHT) DOUBLES AS AN INSPIRATIONAL
OFFICE SETTING, WITH NOTABLE PIECES INCLUDING A
1980S ST. JAMES SIDE CHAIR BY ARTIST MARK BRAZIER-
JONES PULLED UP TO A MID-CENTURY JACARANDA DESK
BY GIUSEPPE SCAPINELLI. A SHELTER-STYLE DAYBED
TEMPTS ONE TO NAP UNDER A PAINTING TITLED L'ANGE
DE L'APOCALYPSE, BY FRENCH ARTIST FRANCIS MONTANIER
(1895–1974) AND SITS NEXT TO A CABINET COMMISSIONED
FROM ELIZABETH GAROUSTE.

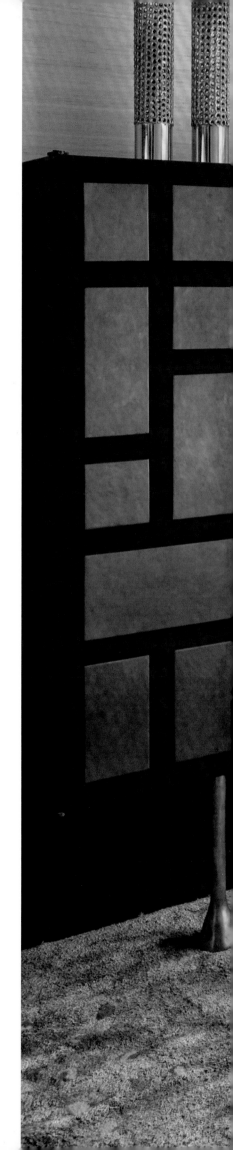

THIS PAGE: THE OWNER'S LOVE OF JEWELRY IS EVIDENT FROM HER EXTENSIVE COLLECTION, WHICH WAS GIVEN A HOME BEFITTING ITS CONTENTS IN THE FORM OF A PAIR OF CUSTOM-CRAFTED CLOSETS, LINED IN RAW SILK AND WITH INTERIOR MIRRORED DOORS. THIS LUXURIOUS SOLUTION, LOCATED IN A CORRIDOR OFF THE MASTER BEDROOM, UTILIZES SMALL BOWLS IN ORGANIC SHAPES, MANY FROM DINOSAUR DESIGNS, TO DISPLAY THESE TREASURES.

PREVIOUS PAGE: A CORNER OF THE MASTER BEDROOM, WITH VIEWS TO THE ADJACENT PRIVATE TERRACE, IS SET WITH A 1940S WING CHAIR BY PIER LUIGI COLLI NEXT TO A STATELY, CUSTOM-DESIGNED MEDIA CABINET IN OAK AND BRASS. THE SCULPTURAL CYLINDRICAL LAMPS ARE 1950S BRASS PIECES BY SWEDISH DESIGNER PIERRE FORSELL FOR SKULTUNA.

NEXT PAGE: ALMOST EVERY SURFACE IN THE MASTER BATH IS COVERED IN PALISSANDRO TIGER MARBLE, A STONE WITH DRAMATIC VEINING THAT RESEMBLES A FLAME STITCH. IT IS SOFTENED BY A CUSTOM FLOOR STOOL UPHOLSTERED IN CURLY LAMB'S WOOL, WITH SOLID BRONZE FEET. OTHER NOTABLE PIECES INCLUDE A JEAN PERZEL PLAFONNIER CEILING FIXTURE, 1970S MURANO GLASS SCONCES, AND CUSTOM WALL MIRRORS.

THE MASTER BATH IS A TEMPLE OF HONED PALISSANDRO TIGER MARBLE.

SEVERAL SEATING AREAS WERE CREATED ON THIS VERY
GENEROUS TERRACE, TO BEST TAKE ADVANTAGE OF THE ICONIC
VIEWS OF SOHO ROOFTOPS AND THE CITY BEYOND. IT'S A
CASUAL COMFORTABLE MIX OF CHAISE LOUNGES, ARMCHAIRS,
AND SEVERAL CUSTOM MARBLE PIECES. A LESS OBVIOUS
ARCHITECTURAL ELEMENT IS THE RELATIONSHIP BETWEEN
THE PATTERN OF THE GRANITE PAVERS IN THIS SPACE,
REFLECTED IN THE MIRRORED RAILING, AND THE TROMPE
L'OEIL STRIPED WALLPAPER THAT LINES THE INTERIOR
STAIRCASE, BRINGING THE INSIDE OUT, AND VICE VERSA.

Passion Project

Welcome to the current incarnation of the Wearstler-Korzen residence, our family's home for the past fifteen years. Originally built in 1926 as a Spanish Colonial Revival, it was remodeled five years later by "architect to the stars" James E. Dolena in a classic Georgian style. We bought it from the Broccoli family (Cubby Broccoli created and produced the James Bond films), but had to reassure them that we wouldn't tear it down. We did embark upon an extensive renovation of all structures on the property, including the pool and gardens, and added a wing onto the home to accommodate the needs of our family. We were intent on preserving the historical integrity of the home, and took steps to ensure it was listed as a historic property and protected going forward.

It is truly magnificent, with several smaller structures, including a guesthouse and pool house that was once used as a cinema. The two-story main house retains many original, refined details, from the intricate Georgian, Federal, and Neoclassical moldings, to the handsome marble bathrooms and even the solid, boiserie paneled doors. Viewed from above, the house is a square shape with an internal courtyard that can be seen from almost every room in the home, which often makes it feel like we're living in a tree house.

The interiors have, of course, evolved, as I discover and fall in love with new artists and artisans every day, and use our home as my creative laboratory to experiment with their works. My eye has become more educated and refined with time, and I actively seek out pieces that are unusual or rare—the anomalies of the world—to create a global assemblage of unique and important pieces of furniture, furnishings, and art. It remains true to my belief in mixing styles, eras, and mediums, bringing together the stars of the past with today's emerging artists to create environments—indoors and out—that are at once inviting, comfortable, and evocative.

OUR HOME DATES TO 1926, AND FEATURES A LANDSCAPED INTERIOR
COURTYARD (ABOVE) WITH MAJESTIC CYPRESS TREES AND MANICURED
GREENERY, WHICH CAN BE SEEN FROM MOST ROOMS. A PERIOD-
APPROPRIATE SKYLIGHT WAS ADDED TO THE ENTRYWAY (RIGHT): AN
INTERESTING ARCHITECTURAL DETAIL THAT SHEDS NATURAL LIGHT
INTO THE ROTUNDA, ILLUMINATING A SCULPTURAL METAL CHAIR
FROM THE 1980S, A CIRCULAR TABLE BY JORDANIAN ARTISTS, AND
A LOUIS DUROT MIRROR.

THIS PAGE: THE ALTERNATING BLACK-AND-WHITE STRIPES OF MY LINEAGE CHAIR, CRAFTED FROM HONED NERO MARQUINA AND WHITE MARBLE, STANDS IN STARK CONTRAST WITH THE HOME'S PERIOD MOLDINGS ON THE WALL IT'S SET AGAINST, BUT SIMULTANEOUSLY ECHOES THEIR HORIZONTAL LINES. ITS ANGULAR SHAPE SPEAKS TO THE GEOMETRY OF THE STONE FLOOR OF THE ROTUNDA, A COMBINATION OF MARBLES (ARABESCATO CARRARA, NERO MARQUINA AND ITALIAN VERDE), WITH COLORS CHOSEN TO MIMIC THOSE FOUND IN THE COURTYARD JUST OUTSIDE THIS AREA.

PREVIOUS PAGE: WHAT A POWDER ROOM LACKS IN SPACE, IT MAKES UP FOR IN TOP-TO-BOTTOM STYLE, BEGINNING WITH THE BRUSHED BRASS MINIMALIST ARETI PLATE AND SPHERE LIGHT FIXTURE, A PLASTER TABLE BY ELS WOLDHEK AND GEORGI MANASSIEV OF ODD MATTER STUDIO, FASHIONED TO LOOK LIKE AN EXOTIC ANCIENT STONE, AND A WHITE ACETONE EROSIONS CHAIR BY TORONTO-BASED DESIGN FIRM SUSAN FOR SUSAN. THE WHITE CABINETRY IS ORIGINAL TO THE HOME, AND THE FLOORING IS THE SAME STONE AND PATTERN I USED IN THE ADJACENT FOYER AREA.

NEXT PAGE: THE HOME WAS ORIGINALLY BUILT IN 1926 AS A SPANISH COLONIAL REVIVAL. A LITTLE OVER A DECADE LATER, THE OWNERS TAPPED JAMES E. DOLENA, WHO WAS KNOWN AS THE "ARCHITECT TO THE STARS" TO RENOVATE IT. THE RESULTING GEORGIAN STYLE HOME, WHICH HAS HAD ONLY FOUR OWNERS (INCLUDING CAROLE LOMBARD), FEATURES INCREDIBLE PERIOD DETAILS LIKE THESE MOLDINGS AND IS NOW LISTED AS A HISTORIC HOME.

AN ANGULAR, VINTAGE DOLORES CHAIR (ABOVE) BY DUTCH
DESIGNER ROB ECKHARDT IS ONE OF A PAIR IN THE LIVING
ROOM. AN ADJACENT CORNER OF THAT SAME, LIGHT-FILLED
ROOM HOUSES A MID-CENTURY FRENCH CREDENZA WITH
DOORS PAINTED WHITE AND BLACK SET UNDERNEATH A
PAINTING BY LOS ANGELES- AND BOISE-BASED ARTIST
LEN KLIKUNAS, AND A SCULPTURAL LEATHER BENCH, WITH
VERY 1980S CURVES, BY AN UNKNOWN ARTIST.

THIS PAGE: A LOFTY, ARCHED, AND DIVIDED LIGHT PICTURE WINDOW PROVIDES VIEWS OF THE LANDSCAPED COURTYARD; THE LUSH SHADES OF GREEN OUTDOORS MAKE A WONDERFUL BACKDROP FOR THE SCULPTURE BY KIM NELSON AND OUT LINE BENCH BY GUROVICI GHERMAN.

PREVIOUS PAGE: THE LIVING ROOM WAS LEFT LARGELY INTACT WITH THE EXCEPTION OF THE BLACK MARBLE FIREPLACE, WHICH WE ADDED. IT OCCUPIES A PLACE OF HONOR DIRECTLY OPPOSITE A LARGE, PLATEGLASS WINDOW, WHICH OFFERS VIEWS OF THE POOL, POOL HOUSE, MANICURED GARDEN, AND ICONIC LOS ANGELES PALM TREES. FURNISHINGS AND LIGHTING CHOSEN FOR THIS SPACE SPAN DECADES AND STYLE ERAS, FROM CONTEMPORARY SOFAS TO VINTAGE EUROPEAN PIECES FROM THE '50S, '60S, AND '80S, ACCENTED BY CAREFULLY CHOSEN WORKS OF ART.

WHILE THE HOUSE, AT FOURTEEN-THOUSAND SQUARE FEET, IS VAST, IT
HAS ONLY TWO STORIES, WHICH ARE ACCESSED BY MULTIPLE STAIRCASES.
THIS ONE IS BY FAR THE GRANDEST, A SWEEPING STRUCTURE FEATURING
CURVACEOUS IRONWORK TYPICAL OF THE GEORGIAN ERA. THE GRAPHIC RUNNER
WAS A CUSTOM DESIGN CREATED SPECIFICALLY FOR THIS STAIRCASE, AND
AVAILABLE THROUGH THE RUG COMPANY; THE NERO MARQUINA MARBLE TABLE
IS A VINTAGE PIECE.

THIS PAGE: THE MUSIC ROOM—SO NAMED FOR THE RECORD PLAYER AND COLLECTION OF VINTAGE VINYL HOUSED WITHIN—IS ONE OF THE MORE INTIMATE SPACES IN OUR HOME, YET ANCHORED BY A PAIR OF BOLD, RED CLUB CHAIRS BY VLADIMIR KAGAN, FLANKING A TABLE BY LOS ANGELES—BASED ARTIST GARRY KNOX BENNETT. THE ROSA ALICANTE MARBLE TOP OF PELLE STUDIO'S LOST & FOUND TABLE SEEMS TO FLOAT OVER ITS RADIAL PATTERN OF SOLID BRASS SUPPORTS. TO ITS LEFT SITS A WRINKLED STOOL BY OMAHA—BASED ARTIST CHRISTOPHER PRINZ.

PREVIOUS PAGE: A PAIR OF 1970S SCANDINAVIAN LAMPS CAST A WARM GLOW FROM THEIR SPOT ATOP A VINTAGE CABINET FROM THE FOLLOWING DECADE.

THE GARDEN ROOM IS SO NAMED AS IT CANTILEVERS OUT TO THE OUTDOORS,
INTO A VERITABLE FOREST OF FRAGRANT EUCALYPTUS TREES, GIVING
THE EFFECT OF LOUNGING IN A TREE HOUSE. THE WOOD PANELING IS
ORIGINAL TO THE HOME, BUT NOW PAINTED THE COLOR OF TREE TRUNKS,
TO STYLISTICALLY DIALOGUE WITH THE LANDSCAPE. A PAIR OF VINTAGE
LOUNGE CHAIRS BY DANISH DESIGNER ILLUM WIKKELSO (LEFT) OCCUPIES A
PRIME SPOT BESIDE A ROBERT ROESCH SCULPTURE; THE CABINET (RIGHT)
IS AN IVES CONSOLE I DESIGNED USING EBONIZED OAK AND MARBLE LEGS.

THIS PAGE: THE BUTLER'S KITCHEN, SEEN OVERFLOWING WITH FLOWERS IN PREPARATION FOR A FETE, HAS BUILT-IN CUSTOM CABINETRY PAINTED A RICH SHADE OF BLUE (PRATT & LAMBERT'S BLUE SPRUCE), AND A VIBRANT, ALMOST ELECTRIC GREEN ONYX COUNTERTOP. THIS IS WHERE I RETREAT FOR A FEW MOMENTS OF "ME TIME" EVERY MORNING—WHERE I'LL HAVE MY COFFEE, CATCH UP ON THE NEWS, AND TAKE IN THE BEAUTIFUL VIEW OF THE EUCALYPTUS TREES OUTSIDE.

NEXT PAGE: A PAIR OF UTRECHT CHAIRS BY DUTCH ARCHITECT GERRIT RIETVELD IN THE POWDER ROOM VESTIBULE; THEY HAVE BEEN UPHOLSTERED IN MY GEOMETRIC "DISTRICT" FABRIC.

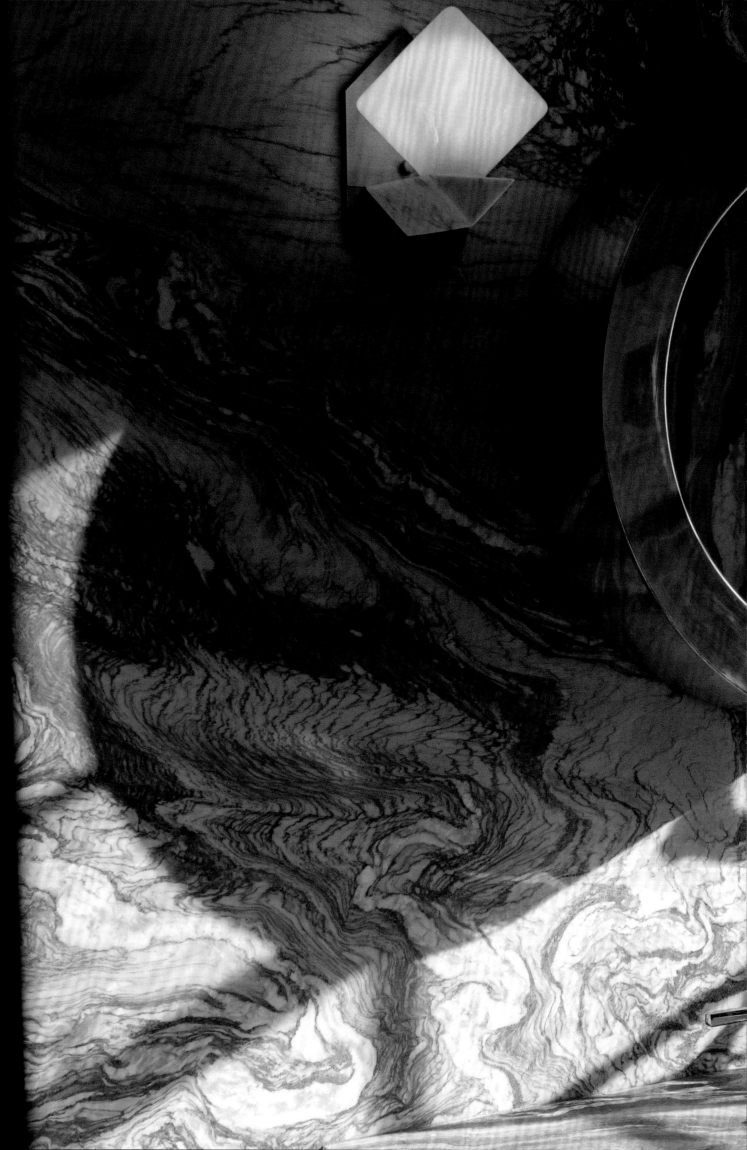

(LEFT) A VINTAGE CERAMIC TABLE WITH TRUNKLIKE BASE IS SET WITH A
COMBINATION OF CHAIRS, INCLUDING 1960S STYLES FROM THE PARIS FLEA
MARKET AND MY SONNET CHAIR, UPHOLSTERED IN A FUN, TEXTURAL GOAT
HAIR. THE RUG IS SCANDINAVIAN, THE PLASTER LIGHT FIXTURE IS A
CONTEMPORARY PIECE BY ENTLER STUDIO IN LOS ANGELES, AND THE MIRROR
IS BY BRITISH DESIGNER LEE BROOM. (ABOVE) A FANCIFUL 1990S CABINET
BY AN UNKNOWN ARTIST IS SET IN CONVERSATION WITH A STOOL FROM
LONDON-BASED STUDIO ILIO'S "HOT WIRE EXTENSION" SERIES.

WE CUSTOM DESIGNED AND FABRICATED OUR
KITCHEN WITH STAINLESS STEEL CABINETRY
AND SOLID BRASS TRIM.

(ABOVE) SHAPES FROM TRADITIONAL KOREAN POTTERY AND CONTEMPORARY
SCANDINAVIAN DINNERWARE INSPIRED THIS DINNER SETTING BY
ARIZONA-BASED CERAMIC ARTIST SAM CHUNG, SHOWN WITH CLASSIC
JOSEF HOFFMANN BARWARE. (RIGHT) FAYE TOOGOOD'S PUFFBALL PENDANT
LAMP PRESIDES OVER MY FRACTURED GLASS DINING TABLE, SO NAMED
BECAUSE EACH PANEL OF TEMPERED GLASS IS HAND FRACTURED AND
BANDED BY BRASS. ELLIOTT DINING CHAIRS, ALSO OF MY DESIGN, ARE
SET AT THE TABLE; A LOUIS DUROT SPIRAL CHAIR IS AT LEFT, UNDER
A TOBIA SCARPA FOGLIO SCONCE.

THIS PATINATED BRASS CABINET, WHICH I FOUND AT THE PARIS
FLEA MARKET, IS STYLISH STORAGE FOR THE NEW AND VINTAGE
PIECES THAT I USE FOR ENTERTAINING.

MISHA KAHN'S 2019 BENCH *SOMEWHERE IN THE MULTIVERSE*
WAS COMMISSIONED SPECIFICALLY FOR THIS SPACE. IT WAS
HANDCRAFTED USING CONCRETE, STEEL, GLAZED EARTHENWARE,
AND ENAMEL.

THE ARC OF A 1987 PAPILLION CHAIR BY PROSIM SEDNI
BRILLIANTLY DIALOGUES WITH THE ORNATE, ORIGINAL
FEDERAL-STYLE ARCHITECTURE OF THE DOORS.

A TREE-HOUSE-LIKE SITTING ROOM, JUST OFF THE
MASTER BEDROOM, FEATURING A MID-CENTURY DANISH
SOFA BY BORGE MOGENSEN, A JOE COLOMBO LOUNGE
CHAIR, AND A TABLE BY ROSS HANSEN.

ONE OF MY SONS SLEEPS IN A 1970S FOUR-POSTER BURLWOOD
BED, LOUNGES ON TOGO CHAIRS BY MICHEL DUCAROY FOR
LIGNE ROSET, AND ACCESSORIZES HIS DRESSER WITH A COOL
LAMP BY LOS ANGELES ARTIST GARRY KNOX BENNETT.

OUR PROPERTY FEATURES A BEAUTIFUL POOL HOUSE (ON THE PREVIOUS PAGE)
AND INCREDIBLE LANDSCAPING BY ART LUNA, INCLUDING SOARING PALM
TREES REFLECTED IN THE POOL (ABOVE). PAOLA LENTI'S COUPE—SHAPED
BISTRO PARASOLS SHADE THE KRIOS LOUNGERS BY CONRAD SANCHEZ.

A PAIR OF 1980S SCULPTURES BY A DUTCH ARTIST FLANK THE ENTRY TO THE POOL HOUSE, WHICH THE PREVIOUS OWNERS USED AS A SCREENING ROOM. ALL LANDSCAPING ON OUR PROPERTY WAS DESIGNED BY ART LUNA STUDIO, WHOSE PHILOSOPHY IS "STRUCTURE FIRST, FLOWERS SECOND."

Cast from the Past

The first location of Proper Hotels in San Francisco presented an opportunity to write a new narrative—a modern take on nostalgia with an element of imaginative storytelling through design. This storytelling wasn't limited to interior design; it included all aspects of branding for the property and its multiple dining outlets, from naming of venues to creating logos. As a student I took many courses in graphic design, and obviously have a passion for color and pattern; I relished the opportunity to tell the story of this historic space in two-dimensional, as well as three-dimensional forms.

The building, a 1904 Beaux-Arts flatiron by local architect Albert Pissis, located in the city's Mid-Market district, presented certain challenges. It was landmarked, meaning specific design elements, including the original marble floors, had to stay in place. Others, including paint colors, required city approval. And the soaring, seventeen-foot walls in the lobby were originally to remain blank; happily this decision was ultimately overturned, allowing for the display of art from San Franciscans past and present, gathered from around the world.

The building itself was informed by many different European architectural styles, allowing for global inspiration when sourcing design elements: Cubism, Viennese Secession, French deco, Swedish modernism all came into play. A fictional backstory also informed the design: it is the home of a well-traveled woman who collects art and entertains often. Each space in her hypothetical home is a deliberate balance of different eras and motifs, creating conversation areas that speak to each other while simultaneously delineating personal space for guests. Thoughtful detail and execution ensured the design felt inspired by the building's history, giving it a new spirit without taking out its soul.

THE LOBBY OF THIS 131-ROOM PROPERTY, WHICH IS LISTED ON THE
NATIONAL REGISTER OF HISTORIC PLACES, WAS RESTORED TO ITS
TURN-OF-THE-CENTURY SPLENDOR, WITH ORIGINAL MARBLE FLOORS
(DISCOVERED UNDER LAYERS OF CARPET), MOLDINGS, AND ORNATE
METAL ELEVATOR DOORS. A VINTAGE CARLO SCARPA MARBLE TABLE HAS
ONE EVER-CHANGING FLORAL ELEMENT (AN ARRANGEMENT OF SEASONAL
FLOWERS), AND ONE MORE PERMANENT, IN THE FORM OF A LATE 1980S
ABSTRACT CUBIST SCULPTURE WITH A FLORAL FORM BY PETER CHARLES.
THE LUGGAGE CARTS (RIGHT) WERE CUSTOM DESIGNED FOR THE HOTEL;
EACH BASE IS COVERED WITH A PROPRIETARY VINTAGE CARPET DESIGN.

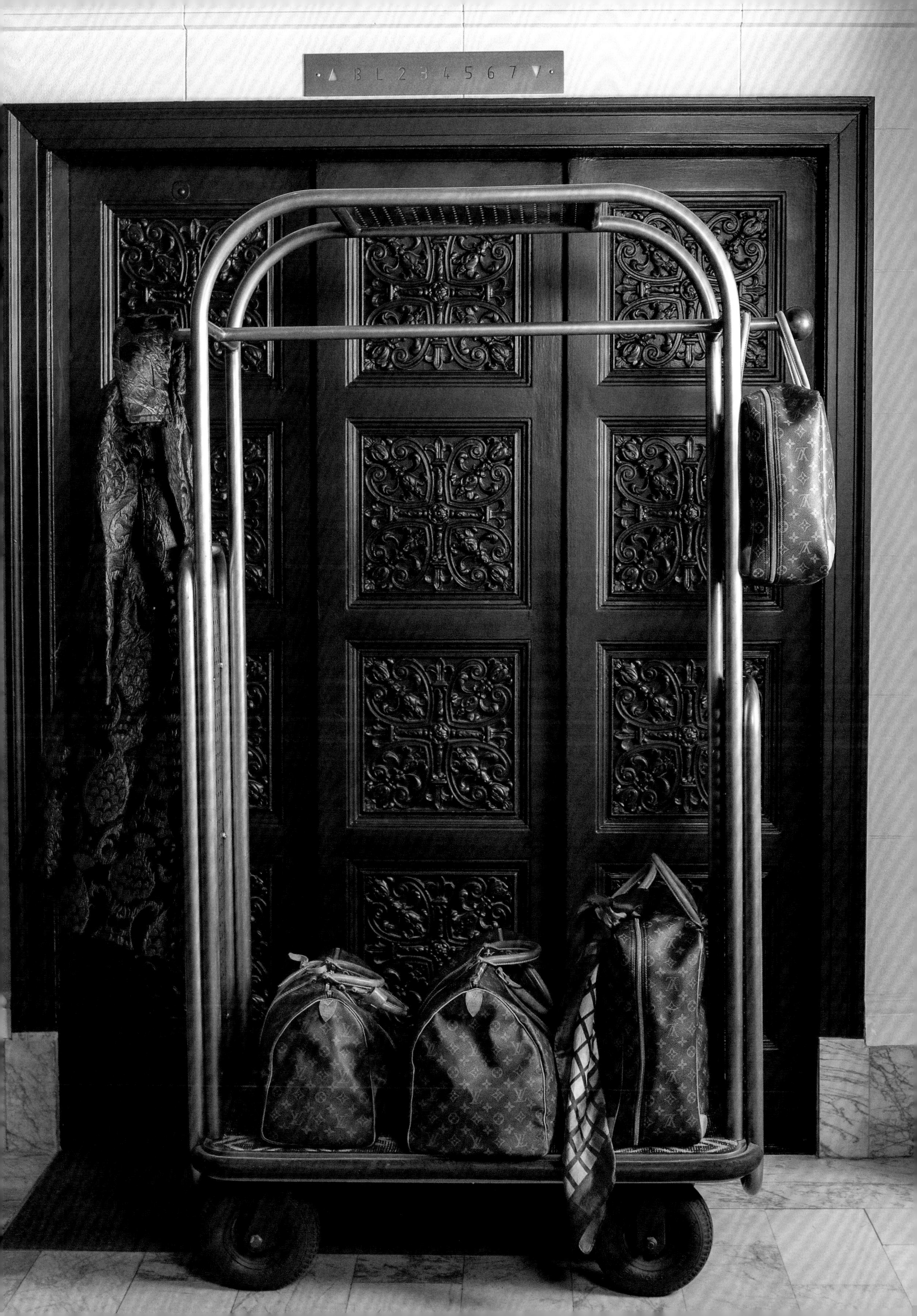
B L 2 3 4 5 6 7

A MID-CENTURY FRENCH SCONCE ILLUMINATES THE BUILDING'S ORIGINAL BEAUX-ARTS-ERA ARCHITECTURAL DETAILS (NEAR RIGHT). THE LOBBY WAS DESIGNED AS A MODERN EUROPEAN SALON, WITH A SERIES OF INTIMATE SEATING AREAS. IN THIS ONE (FAR RIGHT), A 1980S ETTORE SOTTSASS SOFA FOR KNOLL, SET ON AN EARLY TWENTIETH-CENTURY CHINESE ART DECO RUG, MINGLES WITH A VINTAGE PALM WOOD CREDENZA, SET WITH A POSTMODERN VASE, AND UNDERNEATH A LARGE WHITE LEAF MIRROR. A DYNAMIC ROGUE'S GALLERY OF PAINTINGS INCLUDES WORKS BY DAN SHAPIRO, JONATHAN ANZALONE, AND BRYAN FIELDS.

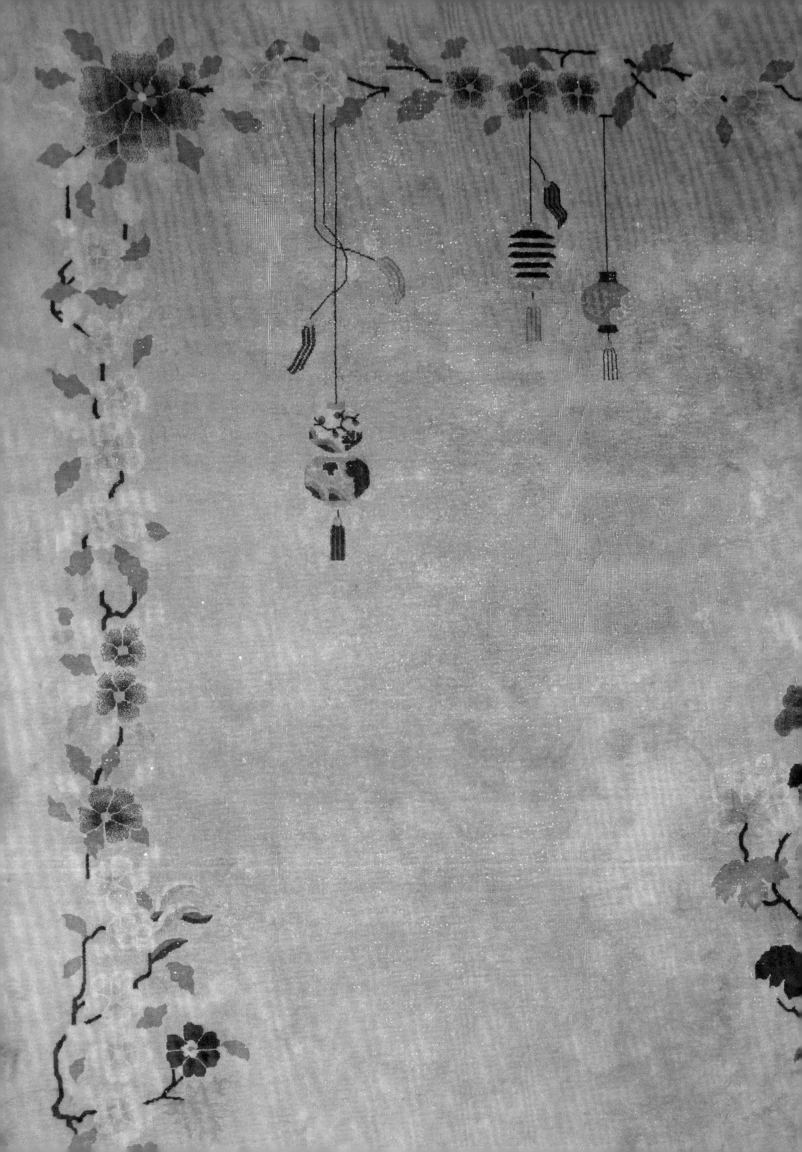

CAFÉ TABLES WITH ANTIQUED MIRRORED TOPS, VINTAGE RUGS,
DEEP SOFAS AND TUB CHAIRS FORM A LAYERED PATTERN PLAY
OF CHECKS AND STRIPES, BRINGING TOGETHER THE BEST OF
THE OLD WORLD WITH THE MOST VIBRANT OF THE NEW, TO
CREATE A WELCOMING RESIDENTIAL SPACE. HERE LINGERING
IS ENCOURAGED, WHETHER OVER COFFEE WITH THE MORNING
PAPER OR A MEETING WITH COLLEAGUES. EVERY ACCESSORY,
FROM THE CERAMIC VASES TO VINTAGE-INSPIRED TEA AND
COFFEE SERVICES, WAS CAREFULLY CHOSEN TO COMPLEMENT
THE FURNISHINGS.

THE HOTEL'S UNOFFICIAL MASCOT IS A LIFE-SIZE GREAT DANE SCULPTURE (ABOVE) THAT ACTS AS A SENTRY AT THE MAIN ENTRANCE, WHERE GUESTS GET A FIRST TASTE OF THE MIXOLOGY OF THE SPACE—A FRESH TAKE ON TRADITION, WITH FURNITURE AND ACCESSORIES SPANNING THE DECADES FROM THE 1920S TO THE 1990S. MOST PIECES WERE FOUND, NOT PURCHASED NEW, AND EVERY ONE TELLS A STORY, AS DOES EVERY PIECE OF ART, IN MEDIUMS RANGING FROM EMBROIDERY TO SCULPTURE, PHOTOGRAPHY TO PASTELS, AND EVERYTHING IN BETWEEN, UNITED BY ONE COMMON THREAD: THEY WERE ALL CREATED BY ARTISTS WITH A LINK TO SAN FRANCISCO.

THIS PAGE: A LARGE-SCALE HANDWOVEN TAPESTRY GREETS GUESTS AT GILDA'S, THE HOTEL'S PRIVATE DINING ROOM. THE PABLO PICASSO-INSPIRED PIECE, IN WARM EARTH TONES, COULD BE CONSIDERED THE FIFTEENTH GUEST AT THE TABLE IN THIS INTIMATE ROOM.

PREVIOUS PAGE: GILDA'S IS LOCATED IN A SECLUDED CORNER OF THE LOBBY—AN INTIMATE ROOM CLAD WITH A LEAFY WALLPAPER INSPIRED BY A VINTAGE EUROPEAN GRAPHIC AND BEAUTIFULLY LIT BY THE GLOW FROM A 1950S STILNOVO CHANDELIER. STRATEGIC USE OF MIRRORS ON THE WALLS AND CEILING OF THIS PRIVATE DINING ROOM CREATES SPACIOUSNESS AND DEPTH. A MÉLANGE OF VINTAGE CHAIRS CONGREGATES AROUND A TABLE THAT COMFORTABLY SEATS FOURTEEN. A 150-PIECE SET OF ONE-OF-A-KIND CHINA, IN A PERSIMMON FLORAL PATTERN, WAS SOURCED SPECIFICALLY FOR EXCLUSIVE USE IN THIS INVITING AND QUIETLY OPULENT SPACE.

Cubist Collage

Villon is Proper San Francisco's all-day restaurant and lounge, named after Jacques Villon, a French artist who was the brother of Marcel Duchamp. Villon was considered one of the most exceptional printmakers of his time and became known for his Cubist works featuring interlocking and overlapping geometric shapes, which inspired the restaurant's decor.

The main dining room combines European modernist styles in a relatively minimal space where the architecture, rather than the art, is the star and dictates the mood of the space. It combines soaring ceilings, wood blinds, walls clad in inch-wide radius ribbed paneling that's been dry brushed for a faux bois effect, framed mirrored panels in Cubist shapes, and a two-toned oak floor in a pattern that speaks to the blackened ceiling.

The anchor of this vibrant gathering place is the nero marquina marble and walnut bar set at the far end of the restaurant and with towering built-in shelving housing an inspired collection of spirits accessed by rolling library ladders.

The overall angularity is softened by Josef Hoffmann pendant lamps with ethereal skirted shades, blackened steel and alabaster Dragonfly sconces by Pierre Chareau, the curves of vintage and custom-crafted seating, and even the Cubist-inspired ceramics, by Mike Helke, that grace every table.

CUBISM INCORPORATES GEOMETRIC SHAPES, OFTEN OVERLAPPING IN
WHAT CAN BE DESCRIBED AS A MODERN COLLAGE. ITS INFLUENCE IS ON
GRAND DISPLAY IN THE MAIN ROOM AT VILLON, THE ALL-DAY DINING
ESTABLISHMENT AT THE HOTEL, MOST NOTABLY IN THE TWO-TONE OAK
FLOOR, THE BLACKENED CEILING, THE RIBBED WOOD WALL PANELS, AND
THE SUBTLE REPETITION OF RECTANGULAR TABLETOPS. THE ADDITION
OF THE NATURALLY CIRCULAR SHAPES OF DINNER PLATES AND DOUBLE
OLD-FASHIONED GLASSES CREATE A MODERN-DAY CULINARY COLLAGE.
IN THE PHOTO (ABOVE) A COCKTAIL IS SET ON A CUSTOM FABRIC;
THE PATTERN, WHICH IS ALSO FOUND ON THE SERVERS' APRONS, WAS
INSPIRED BY THE FABRIC OF A 1930S DRESS FOUND IN LONDON.

NO DETAIL IS TOO SMALL, AS EVIDENCED IN THE METAL-FRAMED INSET WALL
MIRRORS (LEFT), COMPLETE WITH FLATHEAD COUNTER-SUNK SCREWS THAT
LOOK LIKE SMALL RAISED CIRCLES. THE MIRRORS ARE SET INTO ONE-INCH
RIBBED WALL PANELS THAT READ AS SOLID SHAPES OF COLOR FROM AFAR,
BUT WHEN VIEWED CLOSER REVEAL A FAUX BOIS PATTERN. THE MIRROR
SHAPES ARE REPEATED IN THE ONLY ART IN THE SPACE (ABOVE), WHERE THE
REPETITION OF SQUARE AND RECTANGULAR SHAPES IN BOTH THE TABLES AND
FLOORING IS OFFSET BY THE CURVES OF THE VINTAGE DINING CHAIRS AND
CUBIST-INSPIRED CERAMIC PIECES BY MIKE HELKE.

Counter Culture

Located in the iconic "point" of the lobby of the flatiron-style building that houses the San Francisco Proper Hotel is La Bande, an intimate bar and market café. Named after the French word for "stripe," the space was inspired by the French minimalist artist Daniel Buren (who became known for guerrilla public art using striped canvas) and the Secession-era cafés so prevalent in Vienna in the late 1800s and early 1900s, about the same time this building debuted.

The triangular-shaped space, while quirky, provided the perfect canvas for hundreds of handcrafted tiles in a verdant shade of green, which cover the double height walls, as well as the floors, except when punctuated by Buren-inspired stripes of black and white or windows covered in horizontal blinds, creating striped shadows during certain times of day.

Bauhaus-inspired metal stools are set at the substantial counter, the centerpiece of the room, crafted from thick slabs of beautifully veined Cipollino marble. The lighter shades are echoed in the light fixtures, from the Josef Hoffmann-inspired frosted globes to the tiered, pierced porcelain sconces, 1950s Italian designs that look good enough to eat.

IT'S EASY TO SEE WHERE THIS SPACE GETS ITS NAME. STRIPES ABOUND,
FROM THE OBVIOUS BLACK-AND-WHITE TILES, INSPIRED BY FRENCH
ARTIST DANIEL BUREN, TO THE SUBLIMINAL ROWS OF HANDCRAFTED
EMERALD TILES, AND EVEN THE "STRIPE" OF GLASS GLOBES OF THE
1950S ITALIAN LIGHT FIXTURE. THERE IS COMFORT IN REPETITION;
HERE IT CREATES AN INVITING AND TIMELESS MATERIALITY.

Rooftop Reverie

There once was a well-traveled woman who collected art, entertained often, and lived in a Beaux-Arts building. She had a beguiling cat named Charmaine who lived a charmed feline fantasy on the rooftop of the building, basking in the views of the City by the Bay. And so goes the story of Charmaine's, a bar and lounge situated on the eighth floor of the Proper Hotel in San Francisco. It is one of the only true rooftop bars in the city, with an expansive terrace offering panoramic views of the skyline, from Nob Hill to SoMa to City Hall, as well as the building's original copper cornice surround, whose beautiful patina belies its age.

This greenhouselike structure of glass, ebonized wood and brick is a new construction, an addition to the landmarked building that required prior approvals. Many of the architectural details—including the industrial windows and metal columns painted the same color as the Golden Gate Bridge—were inspired by the French designer Pierre Chareau, known for creating Maison de Verre in Paris, one of the first ever glass and steel homes. A curated selection of vintage Scandinavian rugs from the 1940s to the 1960s clad the floors, and the artful interiors, as in other parts of the hotel, draw from the likes of Salvador Dalí (note his iconic "Lips" sofa), Jean Royère, Gio Ponti, Gerrit Rietveld, and Adolf Loos.

There were no limitations to designing this space—excess was encouraged, and led to unlikely pairings that, in turn, created beautiful and unexpected harmonies.

THE METAL COLUMNS (ABOVE) IN THIS SPACE ARE PAINTED THE EXACT
SAME SHADE OF RED AS THE GOLDEN GATE BRIDGE. THOSE COLUMNS,
AS WELL AS THE EXPANSIVE, METAL-FRAMED WINDOWS, ARE SUBTLE
INDUSTRIAL TOUCHES THAT WERE INSPIRED BY FRENCH DESIGNER PIERRE
CHAREAU. EVERY RUG (LIKE THE ONE AT RIGHT) IN CHARMAINE'S IS
A ONE-OF-A-KING VINTAGE SCANDINAVIAN DESIGN, SPANNING SEVERAL
ERAS. THE PATTERN PLAY BETWEEN THE RUGS, THE CUSTOM WALLPAPERS
INSPIRED BY VINTAGE EUROPEAN PRINTS, AND THE UPHOLSTERY FABRICS
INFUSES THESE SPACES WITH A SENSE OF HISTORY AND SOUL.

A SURREALIST PAINTING (LEFT) IS THE QUIET STAR OF THIS SITTING
AREA (ABOVE), HUNG ON A BLACK-AND-WHITE TILE FIREPLACE SURROUND
IN A CHECKERBOARD PATTERN, A MOTIF THAT WAS HISTORICALLY EMPLOYED
IN SOME SURREALIST WORKS. THE BEAUTIFUL GREEN CANVAS DELIBERATELY
SETS AN ACCENT COLOR THEME IN THIS COZY SPOT, SPEAKING TO THE RUG
AND VINTAGE TABLE LAMP, WHICH ARE IN SIMILAR SHADES. THE USE OF
FRAMING—OF WALLPAPER, WINDOWS, AND CEILING PANELS—ALL IN DARK
TONES GIVES THE OVERALL FEELING OF BEING STYLISHLY SWATHED IN
WARM ARCHITECTURAL DETAILS, WHILE ENSCONCED IN A GERRIT RIETVELD
UTRECHT SOFA.

THE VIBRANT JUXTAPOSITION OF BOLD COLORS AND PATTERNS
IS EVIDENT THE MOMENT GUESTS STEP FROM THE PALM WOOD-
APPOINTED ELEVATORS AND ONTO THE EIGHTH-FLOOR SPACE
INSPIRED BY THE VIENNESE SECESSION ART MOVEMENT, FRENCH
INDUSTRIAL ARCHITECTURE, AND THE CITY OF SAN FRANCISCO
ITSELF. FURNISHINGS NOD TO THE LIKES OF JEAN ROYÈRE,
GIO PONTI, ADOLF LOOS, AND GERRIT RIETVELD, AND ARE
ARRANGED IN DISTINCT SEATING AREAS, EVOKING THE LOOK
AND FEEL OF A MODERN-DAY EUROPEAN SALON.

GRATITUDE

This beautiful book is the result of a convergence of many creative talents, from the incredibly hardworking and dedicated team in my studio, to the artists, designers, and landscapers on every project, the vendors whose showrooms and galleries are a constant source of inspiration, and the contractors who literally get the job done. I am incredibly grateful to and for all of you.

For my muses: Lana Gomez and Sebastian Maniscalco, Kim and Amin Cayre, Leslie and Keith Blodgett, and the team at Proper Hotels.

For the creative talents who converged to create the images and words on these pages: Charles Miers, Janice Lau Iwata, Ellen Nidy, Sarah Chiarot, Rima Suqi, Andrew and Gemma Ingalls, Melanie Acevado, Eric Piasecki, Stephan Julliard, Ian Phillips, Manolo Yllera, Francois Dischinger, Noah Webb, Joni Noe, Amy Wilson, Aneta Florczyk, Sophia Moreno-Bunge, and Marisa Competello.

And especially for the love, support, and creative juices that flow from my family: Wayne and Nancy Talley, Tami Kolka, Carolyn Korzen, my awesome husband, Brad, and our sons, Oliver and Elliott.

First published in the United States of America in 2019 by
Rizzoli International Publications, Inc.
300 Park Avenue South, New York, NY 10010
www.rizzoliusa.com

Publisher: Charles Miers
Editor: Ellen Nidy
Design: Sarah Chiarot
Production Managner: Kaija Markoe
Managing Editor: Lynn Scrabis

Texts by Rima Suqi

Printed in China

2021 2022 2023 2024 / 10 9 8 7

ISBN-13: 978-0-8478-6603-8
Library of Congress Control Number: 2019882176

Visit us online:
Facebook.com/RizzoliNewYork
Twitter: @Rizzoli_Books
Instagram.com/RizzoliBooks
Pinterest.com/RizzoliBooks
Youtube.com/user/RizzoliNY
Issuu.com/Rizzoli